Author: Neichole Linhorst
Illustrator: Gregory Green

ISBN: 978-1-7364407-6-6
www.cleverpen.press

For my loves…
Go to sleep!

The Goodnight Fight

When the sun is going down and night begins to fall,

little kids around
the world start
their nightly call.

And there begins the Goodnight Fight, that battle told in 'lore,

when kids get cranky at night's end and then fight all the more...

to steal another glimpse of TV

or play just one
more round ...

but then they find there's no more

time and just go and lie down!

I knew a little boy of 7, so happy and so smart.

One thing he loved to do at night was start a work of art.

"""Mommie can I stay up to finish?
Just One, Ma, one more minute?"

When she said no, he started to cry and didn't try to finish.

And there begins the Goodnight Fight, that battle told in 'lore,

when kids get cranky at night's end and then fight all the more ...

to steal another glimpse of TV or play just one more round...

but then they find there's no more time and just go and lie down!

There once were toddlers aged 2 and 2 — twin girls, of course, who often tried to avoid bedtime by asking for one more course.

After a little nosh, they had to brush and then bedtime for them...And YOU!

And there begins the Goodnight Fight, that battle told in 'lore, when kids get cranky at night's end and then fight all the more...

to steal another glimpse of TV or play just one more round...
but then they find there's no more time and just go and lie down!

And now there's us, just you and me,
and night has started to fall.

We played and learned and laughed all day and sleep has begun to call.

Our bodies need rest and time to recharge, new energy for the day.

So let us not fight and turn down the light, sweet dreams are on the way!

So we ended our Goodnight Fight,
left that battle and went to sleep.

We were cranky at tonight's long
end but surrendered in defeat.

Another glimpse of TV just couldn't win today!

We snuggled down, are snoring loud, and peace is on the way!

Made in the USA
Columbia, SC
18 June 2022